INHALE EXHALE BREATHE
COLORING PAGES THAT SOOTHE THE SOUL

If you enjoy coloring in this book can you leave us a positive review to help us grow and receive a free coloring Book

QUEENS DO AMAZING THINGS

THIS BOOK BELONGS TO

_____

_____

TEST COLOR PAGE

Dream Manifestation Planner

I WANT TO MANIFEST

MY PRAYER

LIMITING BELIEFS I NEED TO GET RID OF

MY DAILY AFFIRMATIONS

ACTION PLAN

Gratitude Journal

Today I'm grateful for

- ....
- ....
- ....

Something that inspires me

....
....
....

Today's affirmations

- ....
- ....
- ....
- ....

Notes & Reminders

Gratitude Journal

Date: ../../....

Today I'm grateful for

- ....
- ....
- ....

Something that inspires me

....
....
....

Today's affirmations

- ....
- ....
- ....
- ....

Notes & Reminders

DAILY AFFIRMATIONS

I AM CAPABLE OF ACHIEVING MY GOALS AND DREAMS.

I AM CONFIDENT IN MY ABILITIES AND BELIEVE IN MYSELF.

I AM GRATEFUL FOR ALL THE BLESSINGS IN MY LIFE.

I AM IN CONTROL OF MY THOUGHTS AND EMOTIONS.

I AM WORTHY OF LOVE, HAPPINESS, AND SUCCESS.

I CHOOSE HAPPINESS AND POSITIVITY EVERY DAY

PROTECT YOUR ENERGY

SAFEGUARDING YOUR ENERGY INVOLVES SPEAKING YOUR NEEDS AND ESTABLISHING HEALTHY BOUNDARIES IN PERSONAL AND PROFESSIONAL ENVIRONMENTS. WHEN SAFEGUARDING YOUR ENERGY, DEFINE REASONABLE BOUNDARIES TO MANAGE EXPECTATIONS AND PREVENT BEING OVERWHELMED BY EXCESSIVE DEMANDS.

Shift Your Mindset and Attitude

Develop a Growth Mindset

Believe in your ability to learn and grow

Develop Emotional Intelligence

Recognize your emotions and understand their impact on your thoughts and behaviors

Set goals and visualize Success

Imagine achieving your goals in as much detail as possible

01

Evening

TODAY I HAVE...
_____
_____
_____
_____

I AM GREATFUL FOR...
_____
_____
_____
_____

I GO TO BED FEELING...
_____
_____
_____
_____

TOMORROW I WISH TO...
_____
_____
_____
_____

ALWAYS You BE

EMBRACE CHANGE

BELIEVE

POSITIVE

I AM WORTHY

I SEEK BALANCE

I AM ENOUGH

I AM STRONG

TRUST THE PROCESS

I HONOR MY NEEDS

ENERGY

n	o	p	s	d	e	e	n	y	m	r	o	n	o	h	i	c
s	r	v	g	h	m	o	p	z	l	i	q	m	g	b	j	c
b	t	r	u	s	t	t	h	e	p	r	o	c	e	s	s	n
e	d	c	y	i	i	a	m	w	o	r	t	h	y	y	m	a
l	d	o	h	b	j	i	a	m	s	t	r	o	n	g	n	l
i	r	a	k	l	y	f	b	u	i	v	f	x	q	k	l	a
e	v	e	r	g	y	u	s	s	t	r	u	s	p	l	o	b
v	d	t	r	l	v	r	z	r	i	m	j	a	e	c	t	k
e	r	e	o	x	w	r	a	h	v	f	p	z	x	g	m	e
z	n	s	a	w	j	y	u	m	e	a	k	e	s	u	b	e
e	m	b	r	a	c	e	c	h	a	n	g	e	n	w	l	s
c	e	z	h	g	u	o	n	e	m	a	l	o	o	b	s	i

Warrior Queen

RESILIENCE WHISPERS, I PERSIST

GOOD
Morning

Be Your Own Sunshine

_____

_____

_____

_____

_____

_____

_____

With the Each new day comes Renewed

Strength and New Beginnings

Daily Mantras to Kickstart Your Day

I am able and capable, strong, and ready to take on the day.

_____

Today, I choose joy, peace, prosperity, abundance over gloominess, stress worry and anxiety.

_____

I radiate beauty, Charm and Grace

_____

I am in control of my mind, thoughts, emotions, and actions.

_____

Today I wake up with Love in my Heart and Clarity in my mind

_____

I welcome positivity into my life today and always.

_____

My mind is clear, my heart is open, and I am ready to embrace the day.

_____

I am resilient, confident and I embrace life challenges as opportunities for growth.

_____

Choose or create a mantra or Affirmation that resonates deeply with you and reflects the mindset or attitude you wish to embody throughout your day. Repeat it to yourself as part of your morning routine, during meditation, while getting ready, or whenever it feels most effective for you. Repeating this can help focus your mind and set a positive intention for the day ahead. Repeat 10 times daily.

INNER STRENGTH, UNWAVERING RESOLVE

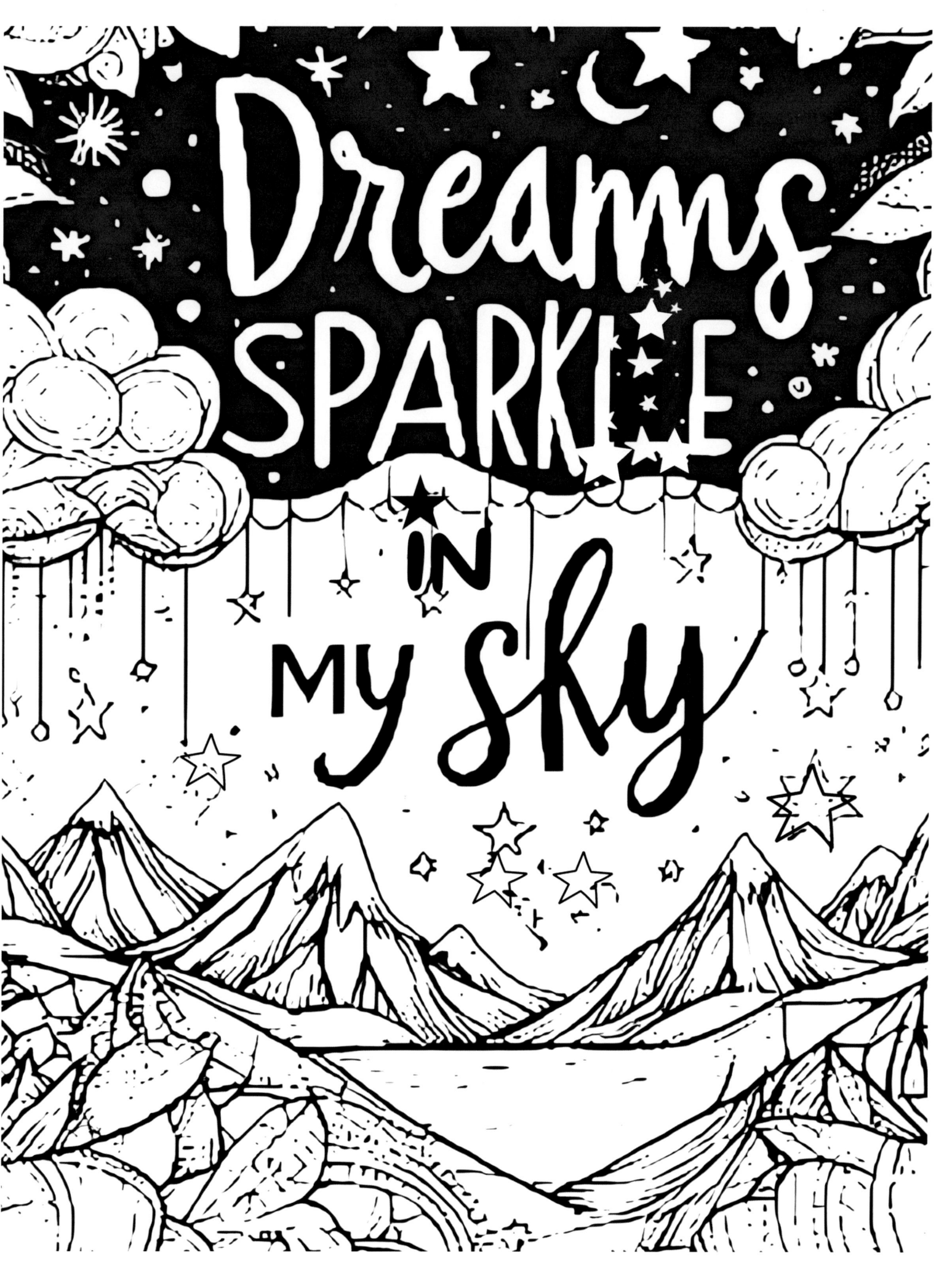

NATURE'S SYMPHONY
LIFE'S HARMONY

Mindful crossword

Across

2. Morning Time

4. Feeling great affection for oneself

5. One of a kind, like every individua

7. My state of being

8. Having inner power and resilience

Down

1. Succesful Creation by way of Imagination

3. To believe in oneself

6. Sufficient for self satiscation

9 To show consideration for oneself

10. The process of personal development

Write a letter of appreciation to yourself

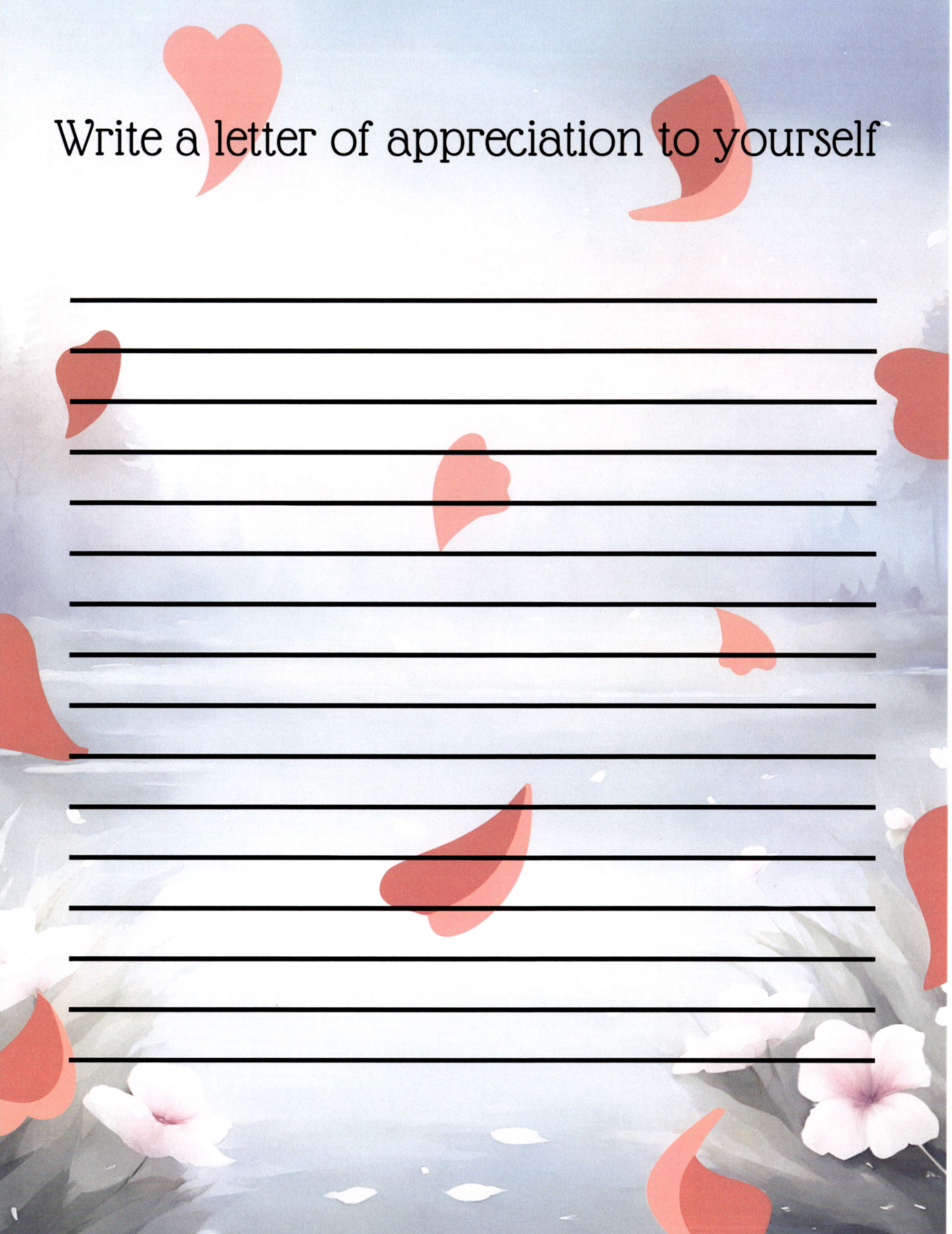

i	i	i	i	i	a	m	i	g	n	i	v	o	l	m	a	i
a	a	a	a	m	t	s	e	r	e	u	l	a	v	i	a
m	m	m	m	a	e	i	o	i	u	j	k	l	i	e	m
c	g	d	p	i	a	m	r	a	d	i	a	n	t	u	h
a	r	y	a	e	e	r	f	m	a	i	l	e	r	l	o
p	a	n	o	i	a	e	w	j	w	d	t	r	y	e	p
a	t	a	d	a	m	c	p	o	y	f	a	s	n	s	e
b	e	m	j	a	r	s	e	y	t	r	v	n	e	a	f
l	f	i	k	o	i	a	m	f	o	c	u	s	e	d	u
e	u	c	i	q	e	r	a	u	u	u	s	w	z	e	l
z	i	a	m	l	o	v	e	l	u	l	h	y	o	i	u

I AM LOVING

I AM JOYFUL

I AM RADIANT

I AM PEACEFUL

I AM FOCUSED

I AM HOPEFUL

I AM LOVE

I AM CAPABLE

I AM FREE

I AM GRATEFUL

I VALUE REST

I AM DYNAMIC

Breathe

INHALE EXHALE BREATHE

BREATHE IN BREATHE OUT

BREATHE IN BREATHE OUT

TAKE A DEEP BREATH

INHALE EXHALE BREATHE

BREATHE IN BREATHE OUT

BREATHE IN BREATHE OUT

TAKE 3 DEEP BREATHS IN

BREATHE OUT 1 2 3 4 5

INHALE EXHALE BREATHE

INHALE EXHALE BREATHE

TAKE A DEEP BREATH

INHALE EXHALE BREATHE

BREATHE IN BREATHE OUT

BREATHE IN BREATHE OUT

Page Protection

Remove to Cover and protect other page while you color

Tesla 3 6 9 Method

write your deepest desire that you want to manifest and see it come true by writing it 3x in Morning 6x in the afternoon and 9x in the evening repeat for 30 days.

MORNING

1. _____
2. _____
3. _____

AFTERNOON

1. _____
2. _____
3. _____
4. _____
5. _____
6. _____

EVENING

1. _____
2. _____
3. _____
4. _____
5. _____
6. _____
7. _____
8. _____
9. _____

Tesla 3 6 9 Method

write your deepest desire that you want to manifest and see it come true by writing it 3x in Morning 6x in the afternoon and 9x in the evening repeat for 30 days.

MORNING

1. _____
2. _____
3. _____

AFTERNOON

1. _____
2. _____
3. _____
4. _____
5. _____
6. _____

EVENING

1. _____
2. _____
3. _____
4. _____
5. _____
6. _____
7. _____
8. _____
9. _____

Tesla 3 6 9 Method

write your deepest desire that you want to manifest and see it come true by writing it 3x in Morning 6x in the afternoon and 9x in the evening repeat for 30 days.

MORNING
1. _____
2. _____
3. _____

AFTERNOON
1. _____
2. _____
3. _____
4. _____
5. _____
6. _____

EVENING
1. _____
2. _____
3. _____
4. _____
5. _____
6. _____
7. _____
8. _____
9. _____

Mindful crossword

Puzzle Answers

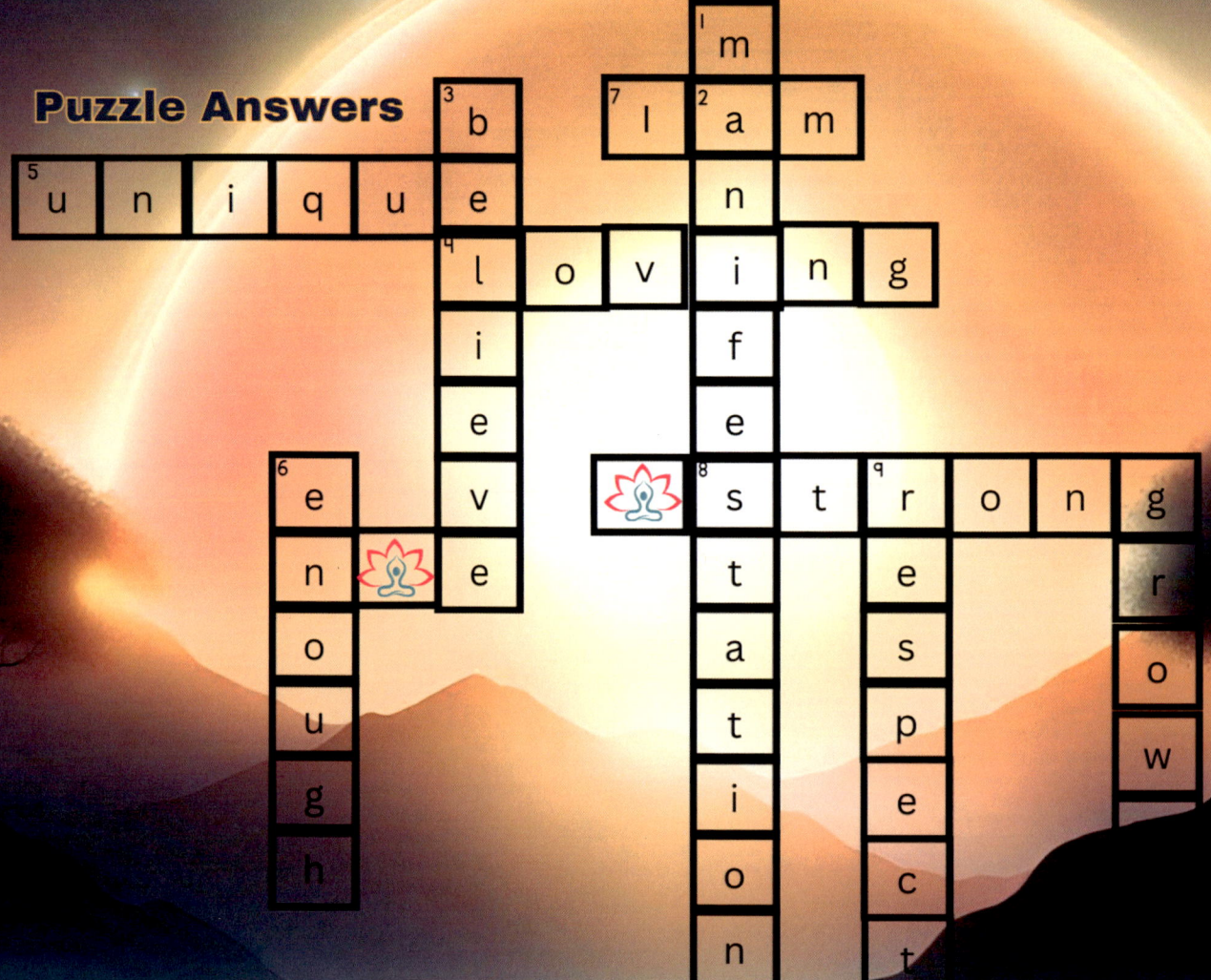

					b		m		
u	n	i	q	u	e		a	m	
					l	o	v	i	n	g
					i		n		
					e		f		
e					v		e		

Across answers:
- unique (5)
- loving (4)
- l am (7)
- believe (3)
- enough (6)
- strong (8)
- respect (9)
- grow (10)

Across

2. Morning Time

4. Feeling great affection for oneself

5. One of a kind, like every individua

7. My state of being

8. Having inner power and resilience

Down

1. Succesful Creation by way of Imagination

3. To believe in oneself

6. Sufficient for self satiscation

9 To show consideration for oneself

10. The process of personal development